IDEAS TO GO

SELF-ESTEEM

D0996129

Ages 8-10

Activities and ideas to develop children's self-esteem,
across the Curriculum

Tanya Dalgleish

A & C Black • London

CONTENTS

INTRODUCTION

Good self-esteem has been shown to be vitally important for children's happiness, social and emotional well-being, and academic success. Mental health and well-being are key themes of the National Healthy Schools Programme, launched in 1999, which encourages schools to play a part in improving children's health. This book provides teachers with ideas and activities to help pupils develop their self-esteem. The activities make an ideal complement to classroom work across the Curriculum. They can be used in isolation, in sequence, or dipped into, as teachers require. The activities will help children to value themselves as individuals and to value the individuality of others, while appreciating concepts such as co-operation, negotiation and tolerance.

ABOUT THIS BOOK

TEACHERS' FILE

The teachers' file offers advice on how to make the most of this book. It offers ideas for classroom organisation as well as ICT tips, assessment ideas and suggestions for parental involvement.

QUICK STARTS

This section offers activity and game ideas that help to promote children's self-esteem. The activities require little or no preparation and can be used across various learning areas to complement existing lesson plans.

ACTIVITY BANK

The activity bank contains 27 photocopiable activities which cover five topic areas: valuing self; valuing others; feelings and emotions; strengths and limitations; and likes and dislikes. The activities can be used in any order and can be adapted to suit individual pupils or classes.

Photocopiable activities

CHALLENGES

These photocopiable task cards offer creative investigational challenges. They can be given to individual pupils or groups, and they can be used at any time and in any order. The task cards involve pupils in in following instructions and completing tasks independently.

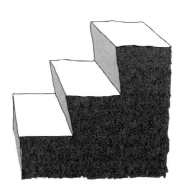

HOW TO USE THIS BOOK

QUICK STARTS

Quick starts are ideal warm-up activities for the beginning of a lesson. Each activity is intended to provide 10–15 minutes of group or whole class discussion. Reflect on the completed task with the children. Ask what they learned and whether there was anything that surprised them.

Example Silly skills (page 13) provides an opportunity for everyone to feel that they excel at something. As an extension activity, ask children to think of story characters who can do unusual things.

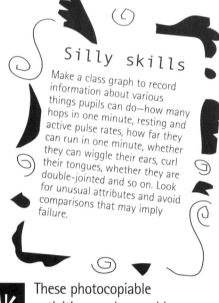

Silly skills

Make a class graph to record information about various things pupils can do—how many hops in one minute, resting and active pulse rates, how far they can run in one minute, whether they can wiggle their ears, curl their tongues, whether they are double-jointed and so on. Look for unusual attributes and avoid comparisons that may imply failure.

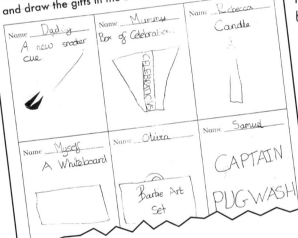

Valuing Others   NAME Sophie

Families

If you could give a gift to each of your family members to show your appreciation of them, what gift would you choose for each? Write the name of the family members and draw the gifts in the boxes below.

ACTIVITY BANK

These photocopiable activities can be used by individuals, groups or the whole class. They could provide the focus for a whole lesson. The activities will not in themselves achieve the objectives, but they will make children start to think about these very complex issues. Many of the activities touch on sensitive issues, particularly for pupils with low self-esteem; take this into consideration when introducing the activities and discussing outcomes. It is helpful to make it clear to pupils whether the activity is to be private or shared, especially for pupils at the top end of Key Stage 2.

Example Families (page 29) could be introduced by sharing with the class a copy of the sheet that you have completed. It is important to accept whatever children write and draw and to listen to the reasons for their choices.

CHALLENGES

These photocopiable activities are perfect for use in learning centres, in the school library or in the classroom. The investigational nature of the activities is in line with National Curriculum requirements and supports the development of investigational problem-solving skills.

Example Friendship book (page 45) can be introduced by brainstorming books that deal with friendship. This is a good way to ensure that books of all reading levels are considered and that children of different levels of ability are able to participate fully.

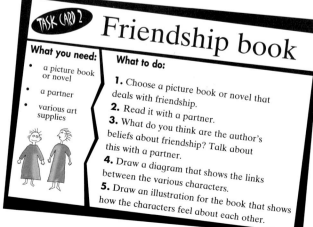

TASK CARD 2   Friendship book

What you need:
- a picture book or novel
- a partner
- various art supplies

What to do:

1. Choose a picture book or novel that deals with friendship.
2. Read it with a partner.
3. What do you think are the author's beliefs about friendship? Talk about this with a partner.
4. Draw a diagram that shows the links between the various characters.
5. Draw an illustration for the book that shows how the characters feel about each other.

TEACHERS' FILE

ABOUT SELF-ESTEEM

Motivation

The most important form of motivation is intrinsic motivation, which comes from within the child instead of being aimed at external reward or praise. Children who feel good about themselves are intrinsically motivated. They are more likely to be successful. For example, pupils who feel good about their reading ability choose to read and therefore become better readers. Success in one area allows pupils to be risk-takers and triers in other areas. The key for the teacher is to find an area in which the pupil excels and use that success as a springboard for other successes. Teachers can use a survey to find out about children's interests and other things they may be good at.

What is Self-esteem?

Self-esteem means how we feel about ourselves. For a child, self-esteem can involve: how you think you are regarded by your family, teachers and classmates; how you feel about yourself as a pupil or as a friend; whether you think other pupils like you or not; and how effective you feel you are in managing your life. Children who feel 'different' tend to have lower self-esteem. If children have negative feelings about themselves, they are more likely to display negative feelings towards others, to underachieve in school, and to develop behavioural problems and/or anti-social behaviour.

Early childhood is the optimum time to foster self-esteem in children; the older a child becomes, the harder it is to counter the effects of low self-esteem. It is important to help pupils maintain a balanced view of themselves, which includes recognising and valuing their own strengths while accepting their limitations. Encourage pupils to set realistic goals. Simply 'to be the best you can be' is a worthwhile goal. If teachers encourage pupils to value themselves as individuals and to value the individuality of others, while reinforcing the importance of co-operation and tolerance, pupils will develop a positive, optimistic outlook on life.

Friendship

It is vital for children's self-esteem for them to feel that they are accepted by their teachers and classmates. Help children to understand that they don't have to like or be liked by everyone, but they do need to accept and be accepted by others. You could model how to give and receive compliments, and demonstrate how you value and respect each child and his or her feelings.

Conflict resolution

Explain to pupils how they can try to resolve conflict. You could introduce children to the following process:
● Articulate the problem
● Discuss possible solutions
● Make a choice about a solution
● Reflect on the outcome

CLASSROOM ORGANISATION

How to use this book (page 4) suggests a range of approaches for using self-esteem activities in the classroom. The activities in this book could also be used in the following ways:

- For individuals during a wet playtime
- In small groups with a Learning Support Assistant
- As homework for a PSE lesson on a related theme
- As a focus for a circle time discussion for a small group
- For paired reading in Literacy
- For individuals working with parents or an older pupil

In promoting mutual respect, co-operation and individuality, it is also useful to consider the parts played by the classroom environment, accessibility of resources and classroom management.

The classroom environment

A supportive classroom environment makes pupils feel secure and helps them to face the challenges presented by school life. Children know that they will be listened to, their contributions will be valued and their opinions respected. It takes time to establish this kind of environment, but the benefits for teachers as well as pupils are worth the effort. The teacher should aim to put aside any personal feelings towards particular pupils and take positive steps to respect and value all pupils equally.

When something positive is achieved by the class, make the most of it by focusing pupils' attention on the achievement. Pupils could write the outcome on a chart for display, for example, 'We worked together to perform the class play' or 'We helped each other learn our spelling words'. Display pupils' work and allow opportunities for them to respond to each other's work, for example, 'I like that painting because I like the bright colours'. Help pupils to develop appropriate language and vocabulary for commenting on each other's work. If possible, ensure that something positive is said about each pupil's efforts.

At the end of every day, try to allow time for reflection. Reflection gives children time to think about what they have done, attempted or achieved. When given opportunities to reflect, pupils learn to recognise and take pleasure in what they have accomplished.

Ways to enhance the learning environment:

- Improve the classroom layout and use displays as visual stimuli
- Select teaching methods and organisational strategies appropriate to the pupils' needs
- Create a learning environment of high challenge and low stress
- Establish a positive, welcoming atmosphere
- Vary the way pupils work – for example, independently or in small groups
- Aim for a balance between structured and unstructured tasks
- Use a variety of learning styles – for example, hands on, visual, oral, written
- Establish the 'big picture' by linking tasks with pupils' experiences
- Use music to enhance the learning environment and to improve the children's ability to recall information

CLASSROOM ORGANISATION

Co-operative learning

Co-operative learning activities encourage communication, collaboration and negotiation. They can lead to a deeper understanding of subject matter, higher self-esteem and greater self-confidence. Through sharing their skills, pupils learn that they are accepted by others and valued as group members. Co-operation can be encouraged through games and group activities such as multi-voice recitation and science experiments. Aim to provide a balance of co-operative and independent activities. Some gifted pupils may become frustrated if they are always asked to work collaboratively; they need also to work on independent tasks that they can pursue at length and to the best of their abilities.

Bibliotherapy

Books can be used in the classroom to help pupils understand their own problems. Children often find it easy to identify and empathise with characters in literature, by relating the characters' situations to their own. Using literature in this way helps children to realise that there are other children in similar positions to themselves. They also learn that problems can be faced and usually solved. If you are aware of a pupil with a particular difficulty (for example, divorce in the family, death of a pet, disability, shyness or bullying), you could choose a relevant story for the children to read, showing sensitivity about why that particular book is being read.

Games

Games in which everyone co-operates and all pupils are winners can play a part in establishing a classroom environment that promotes pupils' self-esteem. Competition has a place, but in games where there are winners and losers, the loser may feel miserable. It is important to ensure that no pupil continually loses or is always picked last when forming teams.

Self-esteem learning centres

A self-esteem learning centre could be set up in part of the classroom or as a shared resource for the whole school, perhaps in part of the school library. The learning centre might contain relevant books, jigsaw puzzles, maths equipment, construction blocks, a listening post, paper, pencils and a supply of art materials. It is a good idea to set up folders of blank worksheets and add new ones regularly. Provide a set of activity cards, some of which could be topic-based and some generic, for example, 'Research a favourite animal', 'Write a poem about your favourite food' 'Work in a group to conduct the following experiment', and so on. Provide activities that allow for both independent and group work. A computer is useful for encouraging pupils to use software collaboratively. You could also provide a book in which pupils can record discoveries or useful tips for pupils working there in future.

Grouping children

Grouping pupils in different ways allows for a variety of interactions amongst them. Groups may be homogeneous (pupils of similar abilities, interests or backgrounds) or heterogeneous (pupils of differing abilities, interests or backgrounds). Smaller groups generally work best because they allow all pupils to participate in the discussion. The teacher can assign roles within the group or ask the group to decide who should do which jobs. Ensure that over time, every pupil has an opportunity to take on each of the roles. Roles may vary according to the tasks involved and particular pupils' needs, but you could use this list as a starting point.

- **Recorder** - makes notes of important points or decisions
- **Reporter** - reports to class on discussions
- **Questioner** - prompts discussion by questioning and clarifying issues
- **Observer** - acts as a witness and later reports how the group achieved it's goals
- **Motivator** - encourages all group members

ICT TIPS

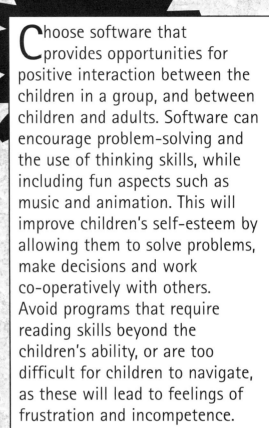

Choose software that provides opportunities for positive interaction between the children in a group, and between children and adults. Software can encourage problem-solving and the use of thinking skills, while including fun aspects such as music and animation. This will improve children's self-esteem by allowing them to solve problems, make decisions and work co-operatively with others. Avoid programs that require reading skills beyond the children's ability, or are too difficult for children to navigate, as these will lead to feelings of frustration and incompetence.

ICT skills can be integrated into many aspects of learning. If computers are to become a valuable part of the classroom, it must be easy for children to use them independently. It can be a help to have a parent rota which arranges for a parent to sit at the computer with children and offer assistance when needed.

It is important to let pupils make mistakes along with their successes. Pupils will learn by trying things out on their own, and by talking about what worked and what did not. Be willing to listen to and discuss what students have done and what they have discovered.

Communication via e-mail can help to boost the confidence of students who are unsure of their communication skills, because there is no need for visual and non-verbal conversational cues. E-mail offers pupils the opportunity to correspond with a wide range of people as they develop their ICT skills. E-mail can be used in the classroom for various educational purposes. Activities could incorporate the following ideas:

● Allow children to e-mail organisations such as charities to ask for information related to projects they are studying

● Set up links with other classes and pupils so that children can collaborate on projects and lessons

● Arrange for pupils to become e-pals with other pupils around the world

ASSESSMENT

Self-esteem can be assessed by observing students over time. The following questions may be useful for assessment.

• Are pupils willing to take risks in their work and play, for example by using approximate spellings?
• Are they confident enough to 'have a go'?
• Are they eager to try new experiences and challenges?
• Are they positive in their reactions to new experiences?
• Do they make friends easily?
• Can they set goals for themselves?

• Are they positive in their reactions to teacher expectations?
• Are they realistic in their expectations of themselves?
• Can they accept defeat?
• Are they willing to learn from their mistakes?
• How do they cope with problems and set-backs?
• Are they confident enough to contribute to class discussions?

Encourage pupils to assess their own work, which could involve keeping folders of their best or most enjoyable projects. The aim is for children to be intrinsically motivated to do their best. Learning to evaluate their own efforts allows them to rely on their own values rather than on outside judgements.

PARENTAL INVOLVEMENT

It is beneficial to explain to parents why self-esteem is important for children's academic success, their happiness, and their social and emotional well-being. Explain that children who have negative feelings about themselves are more likely to display negative feelings towards others and to underachieve in school. You could inform parents that you want the children to achieve the following goals:

• To value themselves as individuals
• To value the individuality of others
• To work with others co-operatively
• To learn negotiation skills
• To appreciate the value of tolerance
• To learn how to make effective decisions for themselves

Invite parents to participate in classroom activities by sharing their skills or knowledge with pupils. Encourage them to share aspects of their cultural backgrounds through activities such as cooking, language, art, music and dance. You could involve the class and parents in community-based events such as Senior Citizens Week.

Ask parents to support your efforts at home by allowing children to make everyday choices such as what the family will have for dinner. In this way parents can let children know that their opinions are valued and respected. Suggest that parents phrase ground rules positively rather than negatively, saying, for example, 'When your room is tidy you can watch television,' rather than, 'If you don't tidy your room you won't be allowed to watch television.'

QUICK STARTS

The great debate

Decide on a topic. Arrange pupils in a semicircle — those agreeing with the topic statement on the right, those disagreeing on the left, and those undecided across the top. Pupils take turns to present their opinions on the topic, starting with one who agrees, then one who disagrees, then one who is undecided. There should be no interruptions during each speaker's turn, and pupils should be tolerant of other opinions.

Pen pals

Organise for your pupils to write to pen pals in another school. Try to organise a school in a different geographic area (i.e. city/country, small town/large town, inner city/suburbs) so that the children can compare different experiences. Suggest that the pupils tell their pen pals about their families, school, friends, homes, including rules at home, and how they spend their leisure time. Suggest they include photos for their pen friend.

Co-operation circle

Arrange pupils in a circle. Ask one pupil into the centre to express or invite co-operation using a word, noise or repetitive movement. Alternatively, two pupils can begin, showing co-operation with each other. Sound or movement must be simple enough to sustain while other pupils join in, one at a time, until the whole class is involved. Repeat, using other concepts like peace, happiness, friendship, trust.

Journal writing

Read a novel to the class as a serial. While you read, pupils should write comments in journals about characters and their actions. Pause while reading and ask pupils to write answers to questions such as 'why did the character behave that way?', 'what would you do in that situation?', 'how can the character resolve the problem?' Journals can be shared with the class, a partner or with the teacher.

Feelings role play

Discuss the emotions of a children's book character. Ask if pupils have felt the same way. Discuss when, why and how they handled it. Choose characters who express their feelings and then do something positive about them. Have a pupil play the character's role while the rest of the class asks questions about the story. Pupils in role can describe what happened before or after the events in the story.

Imagining the future

Have the children write about their future. Ask them to think about what they want to do, where they want to be, how they want to live. The children should draw themselves 10 years from now, then 20 years from now. Ask them to label their drawings, describing where they are living and what they are doing at each point in time. Display and discuss.

Silly skills

Make a class graph to record information about various things pupils can do—how many hops in one minute, resting and active pulse rates, how far they can run in one minute, whether they can wiggle their ears, curl their tongues, whether they are double-jointed and so on. Look for unusual attributes and avoid comparisons that may imply failure.

Self-portraits

Gather resources including works of cubist artists and self-portraits by artists such as Picasso and Van Gogh. Discuss features and qualities with pupils who then create cubist self-portraits—paper should be divided into sections with the top of the pupil's head in one section, right profile in another, front view in another and left profile in the last section. Portraits can be painted or coloured with wax crayon. Display and discuss.

Puppets and props

Collect puppets (made and bought). Arrange pupils in a circle and have them, one at a time, choose a puppet from a box or randomly allocate one puppet to each. Ask the children to create names and personalities for their puppets and to introduce their puppets to the other children. Read a story to the class and have pupils, in turn, respond to the story from their puppets' points of view.

High drama

Have pupils write phrases like 'Not now!', 'Follow me', 'Paint it pink', 'The dog ate it', 'I want to go home', 'Call the doctor', on pieces of paper. Collect the papers. Divide the class into groups. Each group takes three pieces of paper and creates and performs a play incorporating the lines they receive.

Music, art and movement

Allow the children to experiment with sounds made by musical instruments, rulers, pencils, chalkboard dusters or home-made instruments, considering how these sounds express emotions. Provide art paper and mixed media and ask pupils to create pictures expressing the same feelings as the sounds. Have them explore movement, body language and facial expression to express sounds, feelings and emotions. Or ask pupils to express the mood of music through movement using ready-made music.

The rhythm of a name

Movement sequences are created to accompany the number of syllables in each pupil's name (Ben has one syllable so he jumps in the air while clapping once; Jenny has two, so her sequence is step/clap, step/clap). Pupils form pairs and teach partners their sequence; then pairs join with pairs to learn each other's sequences. Group members practise chanting names while performing the movements, then perform their sequences for the class.

No worries!

Discuss children's fears, ensuring pupils are not ridiculed. Explain that people have different things that worry them. List things children are frightened or concerned about, then alongside each write ways that pupils suggest to deal with the problem. Construct a book dealing with one of these fears. Start with a story outline and let the children create comic strips illustrating this fear and suggesting ways of responding.

Compliment circle

Pupils sit in a circle with one child, who is not allowed to speak, in the middle. The rest, in turn, compliment him/her. This child accepts and responds to all compliments by saying thank you.

Or have the children pass a mirror around the circle. As the children receive it they must compliment themselves. Next, pass an object around (tennis ball/ flower). Each pupil must compliment the person about to receive the object.

Pupil of the Week!

Randomly select a 'Pupil of the Week', who will be the class VIP for one week. Display a board featuring this child, with photos brought from home or taken at school, as well as portraits and self-portraits. All pupils should write a positive message or poem about the VIP and display these with the photos. Award a 'Pupil of the Week' certificate at the end of the week.

Living sculptures

Read the pupils a poem, short story or novel extract, or pause while serialising a novel. Divide the class into groups of three. Have groups make sculptures using their bodies to represent a situation in the story or the mood or feeling of what they have heard, and then present their depiction. Ask the rest of the class to describe what they saw, then each group can explain what they were attempting to show.

Letter writing

Pupils write a letter to a character in a book they have read. Discuss what they would like to ask, and what they will explain about themselves.

Pupils write a letter to the author of a book they have read. Discuss what they would like to ask about this book or other titles by the author, what they will explain about themselves and their opinions about the books.

Multi-voice recitation

Children—individually, in pairs, small groups or as a class—can perform multi-voice recitations. They can organise, dramatise and perform familiar poems, chants and songs such as 'Old Macdonald had a Farm' or 'Incy Wincy Spider'. Depending on the effect required to communicate meanings in the poem, voices can be soft, loud or swift. Different emotions—sad, happy, excited, surprised or angry—can be communicated. Sound effects can be added.

Sound collage

Have pupils make sounds to accompany a story reading or telling, or the recitation of a poem. The sounds can be vocal sounds or body percussion. The pupils need to work collaboratively to decide on the appropriate sounds and their sequence.

Reflecting on the day

Each afternoon ask the children what they learned that day, what they did well, what they need to learn to do better, whom they helped and who helped them. Reinforce positive aspects of the day. Help pupils think of something to tell parents. This ends the day with a positive, uplifting focus. The children can discuss achievements in groups or can spend the last 10 minutes each day reflecting in their journals.

ACTIVITY BANK

NAME

Vital statistics

My name is_____.

My birthday is on _____.

I am _____ years old.

This is my self-portrait.

Height_____.   Eye colour_____.

Weight_____.   Hair_____.

Describes self in words and pictures.

NAME

About me

List three things you do really well:

1. _____

2. _____

3. _____

List three things you can do fairly well:

1. _____

2. _____

3. _____

List three things you would like to be able to do:

1. _____

2. _____

3. _____

Describes personal characteristics/skills.

NAME

My family and me

These are my family members.

Name _____ Age _____	Name_____ Age _____	Name _____ Age _____
Name_____ Age _____	Name_____ Age _____	Name_____ Age _____

Ask each of your family members to write
something nice about you on the back of this page.

Depicts personal characteristics of family members.

NAME

I am a friend

My friends' names are:

_____

_____

Ask each of your friends to write here
something they like about you.

_____

_____

_____

_____

_____

_____

_____

_____

_____

Identifies friends and accepts positive feedback.

NAME

Self-portrait

Find a photo of yourself that you are allowed to cut up. Trace around the photo in the space below so that you have a box the same size as your photo. Draw and colour a self-portrait in the box. Now cut the photo and the drawing into strips lengthwise. Arrange the strips alternately on art paper and glue them on.

What do you think of your self-portrait?

Uses creative skills to create a depiction of self.

NAME

Acrostic poem

Write the letters of your first name one under the other down the page. Write a poem that tells something about yourself, starting each line of the poem with a letter of your name.

e.g. **L**oves to eat ice-cream
Unhappy when it rains
Creates masterpieces with her paints
Yells when she is happy

Uses creative skills to describe individual characteristics.

NAME

Good things about me

List three things that you like about yourself in each of the following categories.

Appearance

1._____

2._____

3._____

Personality

1._____

2._____

3._____

Abilities

1._____

2._____

3._____

Which of the things listed do you value the most and why?

_____

_____

Describes self and valued characteristics.

NAME

Bookmark

Cut out the bookmark.
Cut out photos and
drawings of yourself
and of things you like
or are interested in.
Glue them to the
bookmark on both
sides. Decorate with
your name and cover
with clear contact
adhesive.

Identifies things that are special to them.

NAME

I'm an animal

If you could be an animal for a day, which animal would you choose to be and why?

_____

_____

_____

_____

Draw the animal.

Identifies and describes valued characteristics.

NAME

My family

These are my family members.
Write the names of your family members on the lines. Next to the names write the best thing about that person.

Name	Best thing about them
_____	_____
_____	_____
_____	_____
_____	_____
_____	_____
_____	_____
_____	_____

Identifies positive features and characteristics in others.

NAME

My friend

Choose one of your friends. Write a description of the ways in which your friend is special to you.

_____

_____

_____

_____

Show your friend what you have written. Ask your friend to write comments about what you have written on the lines below.

_____

_____

_____

_____

Describes feelings for others and accepts feedback.

NAME

Interviewing

Interview five people and ask them to define the term 'friendship'. Write their responses on the lines below, then create your own definition of friendship.

1._____

_____

2._____

_____

3._____

_____

4._____

_____

5._____

_____

My definition of friendship:

_____

_____

_____

_____

Begins to define personal relationships and listens to others' definitions.

NAME

Families

If you could give a gift to each of your family members to show your appreciation of them, what gift would you choose for each? Write the name of the family members and draw the gifts in the boxes below.

Name _____	Name _____	Name _____
Name _____	Name _____	Name _____

Begins to indentify things that are special to others.

NAME

Collage

Use magazine images and words to create a collage that depicts friendship.

Uses creative skills to illustrate relationship concepts.

NAME

Feelings

Label each cartoon with a word from the box

excited	angry
sad	frightened
lonely	happy

Choose one cartoon to act out with a friend and perform for your class.

Links emotions to expressions and situations.

How would you feel?

Imagine that you are a new pupil at your school. How would you feel on the first day?

_____

_____

_____

_____

List ways to make a new pupil feel welcome.

_____

_____

_____

_____

_____

Imaginatively puts self in the place of another.

Welcome letter

Write a letter to welcome a new pupil to your school. Explain the school rules and give information that will help the new pupil to settle in.

_____

_____

_____

_____

_____

_____

_____

_____

_____

_____

_____

_____

_____

_____

_____

_____

_____

_____

Imaginatively puts self in the place of another.

How I feel

Complete the following sentences:

1. I feel angry when _____

_____

_____

2. I feel jealous when _____

_____

_____

3. I feel disappointed when _____

_____

_____

4. I am happiest when _____

_____

_____

5. I am proud of myself when _____

_____

_____

Identifies feelings and links them to situations.

NAME

The best thing ever

Write about one of the best things that ever happened to you.

_____

_____

_____

_____

_____

_____

_____

_____

_____

_____

_____

Identifies feelings and links them to situations.

NAME

Who says what?

Write a speech bubble and/or thought balloon for each character.

Imaginatively puts self in the place of another.

NAME

Things I am good at

Everyone has things they are good at and things they may never be good at, no matter how much they try.

What are you good at?

_____

_____

_____

What will you be good at with practice?

_____

_____

_____

What will you never be good at?

_____

_____

_____

Identifies individual characteristics.

NAME

We all have strengths

Everyone has things they are particularly good at.
Write the name of a classmate on each line.

Who can help you with . . .

a maths problem? _____

your spelling? _____

an art work? _____

Who would you choose . . .

for your sporting team? _____

to help with a group project? _____

to share a tent at a school camp? _____

Who tells you jokes and makes you laugh? _____

_____

Who would sympathise if your feelings were hurt? _____

_____

Identifies the strengths of others.

NAME

My favourite things

List your favourite things.

food _____

drink _____

television show _____

actor/singer/band _____

video/film _____

song _____

animal _____

colour _____

day of the week _____

book _____

game or hobby _____

toy _____

Identifies likes and dislikes.

NAME

Things I like

Cut out pictures from magazines to make a collage of lots of things that you like.

Uses creatives skills to depict likes and dislikes.

 IDEAS-TO-GO: SELF-ESTEEM — 8-10 © A&C BLACK 2002

Self-assessment this week

The thing I enjoyed most _____

_____ .

The thing I did best _____

_____

The thing I tried hardest with _____

_____

The thing I need to practise _____

_____

The thing I can do better with _____

_____

The people I helped _____

_____

The people who helped me _____

_____

The thing I am proudest of _____

_____

Identifies and expresses individual likes and strengths.

Role play cards

Work with a partner. Cut out the cards below. Choose a card and act out the scenario for your class. You could make more cards to add to these.

1 Your friend has done something you don't approve of. What do you do?	**5** Some children are calling you names. What do you do?	**9** You and a friend worked on a project together but you did most of the work. The teacher gives you equal marks. What do you do?
2 A child who doesn't speak English has started at your school. Some children are making fun of the new child. What do you do?	**6** A group of children has to complete a group project but they all have different ideas on how it can be done and no one can agree. What do you do?	**10** A friend has created an art work that you think is hopeless but know that she tried very hard with. What do you do?
3 Two of your friends are bullying another child. What do you do?	**7** A friend tells you they won't be friends with you any more unless you stop being friends with someone else. What do you do?	**11** Your little sister is always telling on you. You know it is because she is jealous of you. What do you do?
4 Your friend has stolen something from the teacher. What do you do?	**8** Your mother is working and asks you to help at home. What do you do?	**12** Your teacher leaves the room for 10 minutes. She says that she knows she can trust you all to behave while she is gone. All the class misbehaves. What do you do?

Pupil awards

Name _____

has shown
kindness
and tolerance
towards others.

Signed _____

Date _____

Name _____

has shown an
ability to resolve
disputes.

Signed _____

Date _____

Name _____

has participated
well in

_____

_____

Signed _____

Date _____

Name _____

can solve problems
for him/herself.

Signed _____

Date _____

Awarded to

_____

for _____

Signed _____

CHALLENGES

Perform a play

What you need:

- a picture book
- a partner

What to do:

1. Find a picture book in your class or school library in which the characters express strong feelings and emotions.
2. Read the book with a partner and discuss the feelings that the characters had.
3. Prepare the story as a play. Decide how many people you need to play the parts of the characters.
4. Decide if you need a narrator to tell the audience things that the characters cannot.
5. Choose classmates to help perform the play. Rehearse and perform for the class.
6. Work with a partner. Imagine that you are theatre critics present at the performance. Write a review of the performance for a local newspaper.

Friendship book

What you need:

- a picture book or novel
- a partner
- various art supplies

What to do:

1. Choose a picture book or novel that deals with friendship.

2. Read it with a partner.

3. What do you think are the author's beliefs about friendship? Talk about this with a partner.

4. Draw a diagram that shows the links between the various characters.

5. Draw an illustration for the book that shows how the characters feel about each other.

A friendly advertisement

What you need:

- video camera
- video recorder
- note book

What to do:

1. Choose a song that has a tune with which you are very familiar, for example, 'Old Macdonald had a Farm'. Write a new set of lyrics to accompany the tune (e.g., 'My friend is so good to me, yes oh yes oh yes'). Write about friendship in general or about your view of friendship in particular.

2. Teach your song to a number of friends and sing it to your class.

3. Work with two or three friends to design a television advertisement to promote the value of friendship. Consider why people need friends and how you will promote this in your advertisement. You may wish to use your friendship song in your advertisement or you could make up a jingle to accompany the advertisement. Rehearse and perform the advertisement for your class.

4. Ask class members for feedback about whether they felt the advertisement would successfully promote friendship or not. Revise your advertisement if necessary.

5. Videotape a performance of the advertisement to view for yourselves.

6. View the advertisement and assess for yourself whether it would be successful. Write your comments in a note book.

Freeze frames

What you need:

- other group members

What to do:

1. Choose a poem or story that you know well and create a series of freeze frames to represent the story. Freeze frames are moments frozen in time that are shown to an audience in sequence. You will need to consider gesture, body language and facial expression.

2. When you have finished rehearsing, present your frames to an audience. Ask your audience members to close their eyes while your group sets up the first frame.

3. Tell the audience to open their eyes for 10 seconds to view the frame then close them while you set up the second frame and so on. Freeze frames should be conducted in total silence.

4. Ask your audience for their responses to the freeze frames.

A collage of me

What you need:

- magazines, brochures, catalogues
- scissors
- sticky tape
- glue
- various craft supplies

What to do:

1. Use magazine pictures and words, photographs of yourself, etc., to create a collage that represents you.

2. Attach packaging from favourite foods, streamers in your favourite colours, and brochure or catalogue pictures of your favourite toys, holiday destinations, and hobbies.

 **How bullying feels**

What you need:

- other group members
- various craft supplies

What to do:

1. Work with a group and create a dramatisation that shows bullying.

2. Perform the dramatisation for your class.

3. Repeat the dramatisation but freeze at various moments during the action and ask class members to describe how each of the characters in your dramatisation feels at these points in time during the action.

4. Make a list of the feelings words. Choose one of the feelings words that you have experienced and draw an illustration or create an artwork that represents the word.

 **Playing by the rules**

What you need:

- a partner
- cast members for a play
- an audience

What to do:

1. Talk to a partner. Discuss why there are such things as rules.

2. Write your own set of class and/or school rules.

3. Create a play to demonstrate the importance of one of the rules.

4. Choose a cast and rehearse, then perform your play for the class.

5. Ask your class the importance of the rule you demonstrated and how well the play presented the rule.